Nocturnal Animals

Naked Mole Rats

Kristin Petrie
ABDO Publishing Company

visit us at
www.abdopublishing.com

Published by ABDO Publishing Company, 8000 West 78th Street, Edina, Minnesota 55439. Copyright © 2010 by Abdo Consulting Group, Inc. International copyrights reserved in all countries. No part of this book may be reproduced in any form without written permission from the publisher. The Checkerboard Library™ is a trademark and logo of ABDO Publishing Company.

Printed in the United States of America, North Mankato, Minnesota.
082009
012012

 PRINTED ON RECYCLED PAPER

Cover Photo: Photolibrary
Interior Photos: Animals Animals pp. 12, 13, 14, 15, 18; AP Images p. 20; Corbis p. 21; Photo Researchers pp. 7, 8, 10, 17; Photolibrary pp. 1, 5; Public Domain p. 19

Series Coordinator: Megan M. Gunderson
Editors: Heidi M.D. Elston, Megan M. Gunderson
Art Direction & Cover Design: Neil Klinepier

Library of Congress Cataloging-in-Publication Data

Petrie, Kristin, 1970-
  Naked mole rats / Kristin Petrie.
      p. cm. -- (Nocturnal animals)
  Includes index.
  ISBN 978-1-60453-738-3
  1. Naked mole rat--Juvenile literature. I. Title.
  QL737.R628P48 2010
  599.35'9--dc22
                                    2009025656

Contents

Naked Mole Rats

What digs like a mole, looks like a rat, and acts like an ant? This unusual critter has prominent teeth and is nearly blind. It is the naked mole rat!

If you have never heard of the naked mole rat, don't feel bad. In nature, the naked mole rat is found in just a few African countries. In addition, most naked mole rats spend their entire lives out of sight. They live in huge colonies underground.

So are these creatures moles, or are they rats? They burrow like moles. But like rats, they are mammals from the order Rodentia. However, that's where the similarities end.

Nocturnal, Diurnal, or Crepuscular?

One way scientists group animals is by when they are most active. Nocturnal animals work and play during the night and sleep during the day. Diurnal animals are the opposite. They rest at night and are active during the day. Crepuscular animals are most active at twilight. This includes the time just before sunrise or just after sunset.

Within the order Rodentia, naked mole rats belong to the family **Bathyergidae**. There are numerous species within this family. However, the naked mole rat is the only species in its genus. Its scientific name is *Heterocephalus glaber*. Keep reading to learn much more about this curious creature!

Bathyergidae *comes from Greek words meaning "depth" and "work."*

Scientists use a method called scientific classification to sort organisms into groups. The basic classification system includes eight groups. In descending order, they are domain, kingdom, phylum, class, order, family, genus, and species.

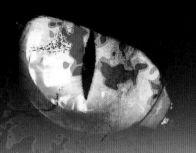
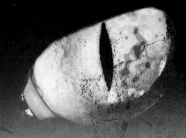

Naked!

You probably guessed one of the naked mole rat's most obvious features. It is nearly bald! Just a few hairs are scattered over its body. You might think this is a disadvantage. But, its lack of fur reduces the amount of **ectoparasites** the animal carries.

This nearly hairless creature has a purplish brown back and tail. Its underside is pink. Older naked mole rats have a more uniform color. The skin is wrinkled and loose. This allows the naked mole rat to squeeze through the tiniest of tunnels. And, it can easily walk on top of and around its friends.

The naked mole rat's tube-shaped body is 3.2 to 3.5 inches (8 to 9 cm) long. Its skinny tail adds 1 to 2 inches (3 to 5 cm) of length. This tiny creature weighs just 2.8 ounces (80 g).

The naked mole rat has small eyes and small holes for ears. Its large **incisors** stick out beyond its mouth. Its thick neck, short legs, large feet, and clawed, hairy toes complete the look.

In Africa, some people call naked mole rats "sand puppies."

Life Underground

Naked mole rats occupy dry **grasslands** and **savannas** in Ethiopia, Kenya, Djibouti, and Somalia. In these East African countries, they make their underground homes. Volcano-shaped dirt hills signal naked mole rats below!

Naked mole rats live in mazes of tunnels. Amazingly, a single colony can cover the area of 20 football fields! Naked mole rats are very protective of these large homes. Colonies do not overlap. And, naked mole rats will fight invaders from other colonies.

Each tunnel system has rooms with specific purposes. These include kitchen, toilet, and nesting chambers. Naked mole rats store food in kitchen chambers. All colony members use the toilet chamber for waste. When it is full, they dig a new one.

In nesting chambers, naked mole rats pile on top of one another to stay warm.

Naked mole rats sleep in the nesting chamber. Unlike most mammals, they cannot control their body temperature. So, they huddle together to keep warm.

Some individuals find other ways to stay warm. They bask in tunnels just beneath the surface, which are warmed by the sun. Then, they return to the nest to share their warmth!

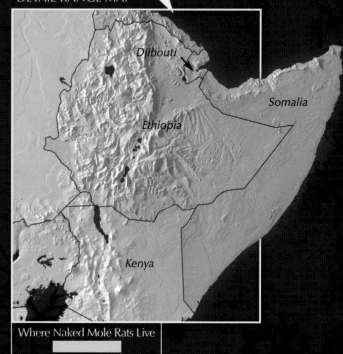

DETAIL RANGE MAP

Djibouti

Somalia

Ethiopia

Kenya

Where Naked Mole Rats Live

Nocturnal or Not?

Is an animal nocturnal if it is always in the dark? Naked mole rats do not seem to act differently in light or darkness. Still, some scientists think they are nocturnal.

Many nocturnal animals rely heavily on their sense of sight. However, naked mole rats have poor eyesight. They rely on their senses of touch, hearing, and smell to survive.

Naked mole rats use their whiskers like you use your hands in the dark. Face and tail whiskers feel tunnel walls and tell these creatures when to turn. Their ears are designed to hear low-frequency sound waves. These are the sound waves that travel best through soil. They alert naked mole rats to danger and even mealtime!

A great sense of smell helps naked mole rats tell predators from food. They know the difference between these like you know smelly socks from apple pie!

Naked mole rats don't have to look where they're going. Their whiskers guide them! So, they can move as quickly backward as forward.

Nocturnal Eyes

Some lucky nocturnal animals have special eye features that help them in the dark. They may have large eyes compared to their body size. Also, their pupils may open wider than ours do in low light. These two features allow more light to enter their eyes.

After light enters an eye's pupil, the lens focuses it on the retina. In the retina, two special kinds of cells receive the light. These are rods and cones.

Rods work in low light. They detect size, shape, and brightness. Cones work in bright light. They detect color and details. Nocturnal animals often have many more rods than cones.

Many nocturnal eyes also have a tapetum lucidum behind the retina. The tapetum is like a mirror. Light bounces off of it and back through the retina a second time. This gives the light another chance to strike the rods. The reflected light then continues back out through the pupil. This causes the glowing eyes you may see at night!

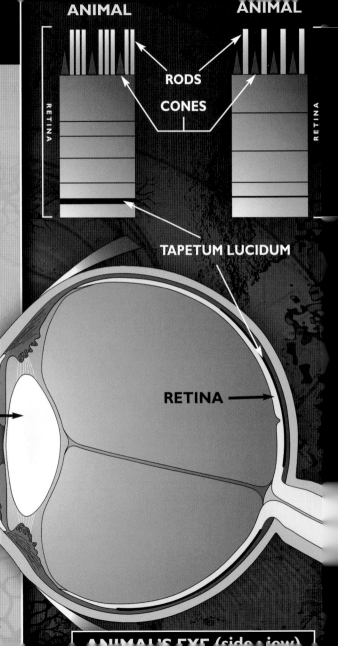

ANIMAL   ANIMAL

RODS
CONES

RETINA   RETINA

TAPETUM LUCIDUM

RETINA

LENS

PUPIL

ANIMAL'S EYE (side view)

Colonies

Digging new tunnels takes teamwork!

Naked mole rats are extremely dependent on one another for survival. They work together to help their colony flourish. This is called **eusocial** behavior. It is rare for mammals, but common for insects such as ants and bees.

Average colonies have 75 members. Yet some have up to 300! However large the colony, the queen rules the land. She patrols the tunnels, walking over other colony members that are in her way. She even shoves those that are being lazy! And, the queen is the only female in the colony who gives birth to young.

Workers care for the queen and her young. They also find food for the entire colony. And, they expand the tunnel system. Lining up nose to tail, a digger at the front uses its strong teeth. Behind the digger, sweepers

Some zoo colonies have two big, bossy queens. However, scientists do not know if this happens in the wild.

push dirt backward with their hairy feet. Last in line, a volcanoer pushes the dirt up onto the surface.

Large, strong soldiers protect the colony. They threaten invaders and predators. Soldiers will make noises, open their mouths, and snap their teeth. If the queen dies, one of them will likely take over her position.

Tasty Tubers

Workers must find food for the colony. With as many as 300 mouths to feed, this is a big job! They spend much time digging for food with their long **incisors**. These hardworking teeth are

Naked mole rats happily share a variety of roots and tubers with their colony.

constantly wearing down. Luckily, they grow continuously throughout the naked mole rat's life.

What tasty foods cause naked mole rats to work so hard? Pizza? Candy? No way! They survive on long roots and fat **tubers** from the **grassland** plants above.

Instead of drinking, they depend on these plants for water.

When a worker finds food, it runs back to the nest. It carries a piece of the food for everyone to smell. And, it leaves behind an

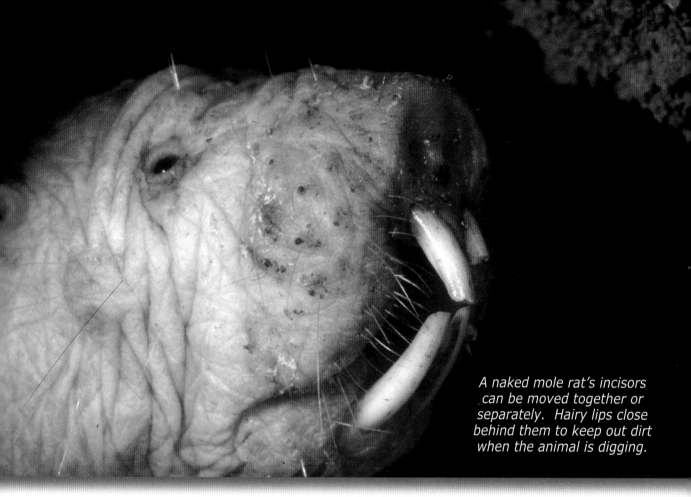

A naked mole rat's incisors can be moved together or separately. Hairy lips close behind them to keep out dirt when the animal is digging.

odor trail. The other naked mole rats can follow this back to the food source.

Naked mole rats hollow out the **tubers** they find. Leaving the outside of the tuber allows the plant to continue growing. In this way, it becomes a reliable food source.

Born Underground

A colony's queen is the only female to mate and reproduce. She chooses one to three mates. Each mate's job then changes from worker or soldier to breeder. After mating, the queen carries her young for 10 to 11 weeks.

When a female naked mole rat becomes queen, she actually grows longer. That way, she can still fit through the tunnels while carrying large **litters**. The queen may have up to 27 young at one time! She can have up to five litters per year. In one year, that is more than 100 pups!

Newborn naked mole rats weigh just .04 to .07 ounces (1 to 2 g). After just one day, their **incisors** begin to show. At two weeks, their ears open and they begin eating plants.

The young begin play fighting at three weeks. They finish nursing after about one month. Around five weeks of age, the pups become even more independent. They help clean the tunnels and carry food.

In the wild, workers may only live two to three years. Yet in **captivity**, females have lived 23 years. Males have lived 28 years!

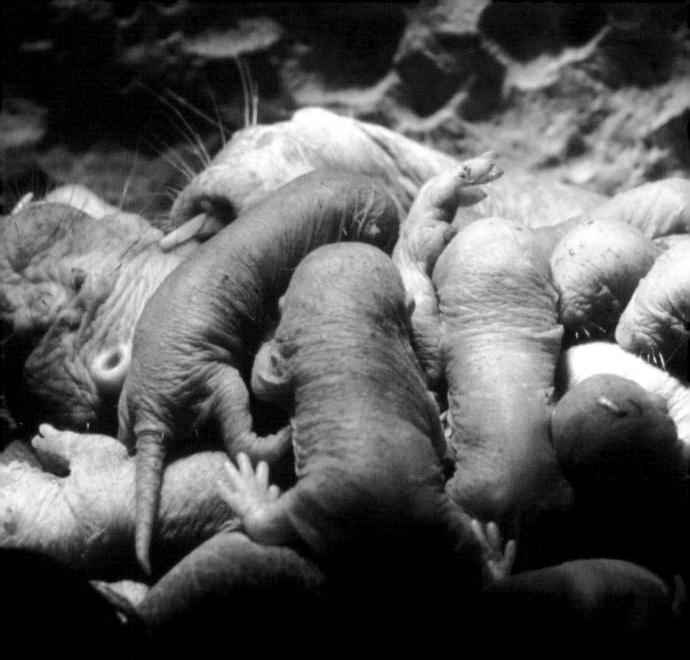

Workers help the queen care for her pups.

Desert Dangers

The naked mole rat enjoys a fairly protected life. Few predators can access its cozy underground home. Yet raptors, sand boas, and rufous-beaked snakes still pose a threat.

Naked mole rats must be wary of predators while digging new tunnels.

The smell of freshly dug soil attracts the rufous-beaked snake. A naked mole rat tunnel system is usually sealed. But while new tunnels are being dug, there is an opening to the surface. As last in line, volcanoers are particularly at risk.

To stop a predator, soldiers will attempt to block the entrance with dirt. If this fails, a soldier may sacrifice itself to save the others. The snake will then swallow the unlucky naked mole rat whole!

In the future, humans could become the naked mole rat's greatest enemy. Currently, human and naked mole rat territories do not overlap much. However, this could change as human populations expand. Entire crop fields can be lost to hungry naked mole rats. In these cases, farmers may think of them as pests and seek to destroy them.

Bright Future

In zoos, naked mole rats live in clear tunnels. This allows scientists to study their behavior.

Currently, scientists are not worried naked mole rats will become extinct. They work as a team to meet their needs for survival. Their homes are safe from most predators. And, they are fast and frequent reproducers.

Naked mole rats have become popular in zoos around the world. Scientists also study these fascinating creatures in their labs. Safe in nature, labs, and zoos, the naked mole rat population is stable.

Did naked mole rats seem like ugly, gross creatures before now? Hopefully, you now see them in a new light. Look for a naked mole rat colony in a zoo near you. There is even more to learn about these fascinating members of the animal kingdom!

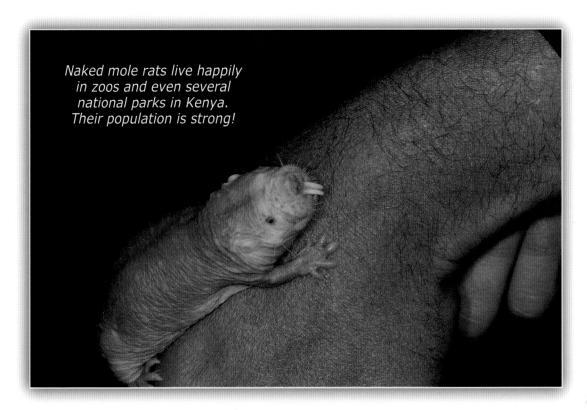

Naked mole rats live happily in zoos and even several national parks in Kenya. Their population is strong!

Glossary

Bathyergidae (bath-ee-UHR-juh-dee) - the scientific name for the blesmol family. This family includes naked mole rats, silvery mole rats, and other blesmols.

captivity - the state of being captured and held against one's will.

ectoparasite - a parasite that lives outside its host's body. A parasite is an organism that lives on or in another organism of a different species.

eusocial (yoo-SOH-shuhl) - living in a cooperative group. Usually, just one female and a few males reproduce. Other group members care for the young. And, they provide food and protection for the group.

grassland - land on which the main plants are grasses.

incisor (ihn-SEYE-zuhr) - a front tooth, usually adapted for cutting.

litter - all of the young born at one time to a mother naked mole rat.

savanna - a grassy plain with few or no trees.

tuber - an enlarged, underground stem of a plant. A potato is a tuber.

Web Sites

To learn more about naked mole rats, visit ABDO Publishing Company on the World Wide Web at **www.abdopublishing.com**. Web sites about naked mole rats are featured on our Book Links page. These links are routinely monitored and updated to provide the most current information available.

Index